May I Only Leave Rose Petals

May I Only Leave Rose Petals

J. S. Drake

Copyright © 2019
All rights reserved.

This book or part thereof may not be reproduced in any form, stored in a retrieval system, or transmitted in any form by any means-electronic, mechanical, photocopy, recording, or otherwise without prior written permission of the author, except as provided by United States of America copyright law.

The information provided in this book is designed to provide helpful information on the subjects discussed. This book is not meant to be used, nor should it be used, to diagnose or treat any medical condition. The author and publisher are not responsible for any specific health needs that may require medical supervision and are not liable for any damages or negative consequences from any treatment, action, application, or preparation, to any person reading or following the information in this book.

References are provided for information purposes only and do not constitute endorsement of any websites or other sources. In the event you use any of the information in this book for yourself, the author, and the publisher assume no responsibility for your actions.

May I Only Leave Rose Petals
J.S. Drake
Tradepaper ISBN: 978-1-945026-49-2
Library of Congress Control Number: 2018966967
Published by Garnet Press
Printed in the United States of America

Table of Contents

Foreword 1
I: An Offering 3
May I Only Leave Rose Petals 6
The Light that can Never be Extinguished 8
II: The Forgetting 11
Fear 14
Wounded 15
See Me 16
Patterns Ensue 17
Blame 18
Being a Victim 19
Dark Night of the Soul 20
Buried 22
No! 24
Stop Hiding 25
III: Adventure into the Heart 29
Love 32
Come Back! 35
Writing is the Chisel 36
Worst Kind of Poverty 39
Wanting More Answers 41
But Why the Barriers? 43
Mothering Me 47
The Loss 48
IV: The Cherished Guest 49
The Pain 52
Soothing the Pain and Chaos 53
The Miracle 57

Growing from an Experience of Non-Love...................................59
But Why the Cruelty?...................................63
V: Befriending the Shadows Within...................................65
Facing the Fears of the Self...................................68
Being Seen...................................70
The Spirit of Play...................................72
Bring the Shadow Sides Home to Reign As the Sun...................................74
Only I Have the Key...................................77
Befriending the Shadows...................................80
VI: Liberated...................................83
I, Alone, Am Responsible...................................86
Forgiveness...................................87
The Angel Behind the Pain...................................88
Rejection is Merely an Invitation...................................90
Projection...................................92
Everything is Within You...................................93
Liberation...................................94
VII: Remembering Together to Bring Us Home...................................97
Infinite Love...................................100
Opportunity...................................101
Builder of our Castle in the Sky...................................102
Allow the Unfolding...................................104
Love is the Language of the Universe...................................106
Every Thought You Have Is a Seed...................................107
What Would Love Do?...................................111
Create from this Space...................................113
You are a Wayshower...................................114
VIII: Our Homecoming...................................117
The Time-Capsule...................................120
Gift of the Rainbow...................................121
Mastery...................................122

The Oasis of Our True Self..123
IX: Of One Heart...125
The Student and Master...128
The Song..129
Of One Heart...132
Afterword...135
About the Author..141

For my immediate family:
We have seen the best and the worst of one another, haven't we? But what makes us so beautiful is that we, unequivocally, see the angel behind the pain.

For all my other family, friends, Gary Acevedo and Rise Leadership Group, and Guru, Louix Dor Dempriey:
Thank you for believing in me always and inspiring me to be the best version of myself I can be.

And finally,
For all those who are and have been alone in seemingly insurmountable darkness and are yearning to find their Light:
You are not alone. You matter. I see you.

Foreword

The Truth

Dear readers,

I wrote this poetry book as a way to cope with the heartbreaks of my life and to connect to my inner wisdom—something that is within each and every one of us. This poetry book is a journey—a journey from brokenness to wholeness, from victimhood to mastery, from darkness to light, from fear to love. Please take this journey with me and know that wherever it takes you that we are in this *together*. We have all been stuck in webs of darkness in one way or another and, for me, this has helped me to discover the truth from the lies. The truth is that I am still finding my way, but I have chosen to share my truth with you in the hopes that it will give you permission to be just as you are and love yourself just as you are. I am not perfect, and, God knows I make a lot of mistakes, but this is me, in the raw—lost and found again and the cycle repeats. One day I think "I've got this!" Then the next, I am falling flat on my face. But I believe the gift in it all is to realize everything is a gift and it's ok to not feel ok! Each and every day, I am getting better and better. Each and every day, I choose to love more than I did yesterday. I am where I am, and you are where you are, and that *is* ok. We all have a purpose and we all can help one another to find our way *Home*.

With love and utmost gratitude,

J.S. Drake

I
An Offering

"Be patient where you sit the dark. The dawn is coming."
- Rumi

"Don't you know it yet? It is your light that lights the world."

- *Rumi*

May I Only Leave Rose Petals

My dear friend,

Through these chapters
I offer you my heart.

It may not always be pretty,
As the way of the heart can open wounds.

At times, my heart is swallowed in darkness.
At times, my heart is bound up by fear.

But *always* is the heart the pure portal to Love.

All I do is choose to let go of the illusion,
The illusion is what is being washed away,
Layer by layer.

How, you ask?

Through countless tears shed—
Like a cleansing rain,
Through screams of rage suppressed,
Finally released—

Like a purifying fire,
Through yearning pleas to God—
Like a breeze opening my heart to
Receive answers.

All is beautiful. All is Love.

So, as you take this journey with me
Into my heart,
So you, too, journey into yours.

May I only leave rose petals in your hearts
As you journey with me to find the Light
Within:
The Light within each and every
One of Us
That cannot ever be extinguished
And
That inherently connects
Us All.

The Light that can Never be Extinguished

Interwoven as part of the tapestry of life
We are born knowing:
We are One.
We are Magnificent.
We are Creators.

Through the eyes of a babe
We know this Truth.
But soon we become disillusioned,
Like a seeping fog…
Pain, fear, and darkness creep stealthily in.

This is the beginning of The Forgetting.

We forget we are One,
Instead, we see ourselves as Separate.

We forget we are Magnificent,
Instead, we see ourselves as Insignificant.

We forget we are Creators,
Instead, we see ourselves as Destroyers.

Through life's trials,
Our Light, forever burning still…
Is buried by Fear.

We bury the Truth so deep
Behind walls made of stone,
For fear, if we look
The Truth will be
That we are Separate.

To face this possibility of being Separate
Is like facing our own Soul Death,
We do not dare look or dig for the Truth,
Instead, we continue living in disillusion.

But steadily it burns,
Deep within our hearts,
The Light that can Never be Extinguished…
Awaiting our Homecoming.

II

The Forgetting

"The wound is the place where the light enters you."
- Rumi

"Even loss and betrayal can bring us awakening."
- Gautama Buddha

Fear

The Killer of Dreams.
The Keeper of Hate.

The storyteller of
Worthlessness,
Not good enough,
Abandonment,
And
Failure.

Fear is a most cunning adversary
Cloaking itself in the name of
Love.

Wounded

Why do you always have to mess
Everything up?
You are so stupid!
You are far too sensitive!
You will never be good enough!
No one likes you!
Wish you were never born!
You are unlovable.
I despise you.

-Words that Birth the Wounded Inner Child-

See Me

Please!
I'll do better.
I didn't mean to…
I will do my best, I promise!
I just want attention!
I just want love!
Why don't I matter?
I just want to make you proud of me!
See? I'm being good!
I love you!
I do not mean to make you mad…
See me!
See me!
See me!

-The Words I So Longed to Express-

Patterns Ensue

You say I'm a screw up,
I'll show you!
I'll screw up all my relationships so severely
That I'll never experience
Intimacy or love!
You say I'm too sensitive,
I'll show you!
I'll bottle up all my tears
And go NUMB.
You say you wish I was never born,
I'll show you!
I'll barely make it by in this world
And contemplate suicide
To make the pain stop!
SEE?
I guess all you said about me was true!
I really am a screw up…

Blame

You ruined it for me,
I was once innocent and free.
You,
With your heart full of hate…
Or was it pain?
All I know is…
It broke us both.
It shattered us into a
Million Tiny Pieces.
How will we ever be
Put back together?

-Heart Pain-

Being a Victim

Life is not fair,
I am not meant to be here,
It's not my fault!
It's not my fault!

Dark Night of the Soul

Dark Night of the Soul,
Consumes the Light within.
Staggering to find my way
Only seeing shadows and death.

My heart in a cage,
I yearn to be free,
Free from this
Dark Night of the Soul.

I scream,
Scream with my entire being,
Yet only a whisper escapes me,
Free me...
Hear me...
See me...
Love me...

Grief pours from my essence,
Yet, it's almost as if
I am numb to it all.
I feel so deeply,
Yet, I am unable to
Birth my liberated self.

Pregnant with potential,
I miscarry again and again,
This Dark Night of Soul,
Lord, when will it end?

Buried

The eyes that used to shine
With radiant light,
Shine no more.

The gleeful giggles
And freeing laughter,
Died long ago.

That creative spark
That could light up
The World!

Buried.
Buried.
Buried.

Under
Harsh words.
Judgments.
Berating insults.
Sickening depression.

The Wonder Child within,
Heart Wounded and Alone.

Buried.
Buried.
Buried.

Waiting to be Uncovered!
For loving arms to embrace and
Bring healing to a broken heart.

You have the key to heal,
To pick up that wounded inner child
And love her like she always
Wished she were loved!

But first,
You must face the fear and pain.
You must walk into the
Trenches of darkness
To find the
Wounded Child,
And Shine a Light to guide her Home.

No!

I don't want to look!
No! No! No!
The gut-wrenching fear
That is buried within…
I'm too scared to dig!
For what if I uncover,
And see that it's true?

Don't make me look!
Let's pretend it's all ok.
I'm ok! I'm ok! I'm ok!

But the fear,
Coiled like a black serpent,
Strikes at the
Most vulnerable parts of me.
Poisoning my very Soul
Like a parasitic Darkness.
And if I do not face it…
I'll surely *never* escape this Hell.

Stop Hiding

I hide, I keep secrets in the dark.
What is it? What is it I'm afraid of?
I peer into the tangled webs of darkness,

The Fear.

Fear Screams at Me,

"You are UNWORTHY!
You are NOT GOOD ENOUGH!
You are STUPID!
You are UGLY!
You are WEAK!
You DO NOT MATTER!"

This darkness eats away at me.
At my Light—my Essence.
I feel so weary, I just want to sleep
And never wake up.
"Just let me sleep…
Just take me from this torture in my heart,"
I say.

As I resolve to just fall away and not take
One step further,
I hear a commanding Light Presence
Speak to me:

"You can only hide so long, beloved.
You are playing hide and seek
With shadows of untruth.
The truth will prevail.
Stop coveting lies and keeping secrets
In the dark!
These secrets you believe to be true.
Ha! These are not Truth!
You are deceiving yourself;
Ye who is a Goddess!
These are sucking the life out of you.
It takes a Soul so much more strength
To hold what is untrue
Than to just be what is true.
Stop coveting the lies and bring them to
The Light.
Do this and you will once again
See they are false.
Anything held in the Light long enough
Becomes the Light,
And all that is not of the Light
Falls away.
And you, who is made of stardust,

Are of the Light!
So, do not fear, because all that will
Fall away is illusion,
And you will find your way Home
Once again."

-Heart to Heart with God-

III

Adventure into the Heart

*"The greatest adventure you will ever take
is the journey into your own heart."*
- Louix Dor Dempriey

"Let us carve gems out of our stony hearts and let them light our path to love."

— *Rumi*

Love

The lifeline of our life.
The degree to which we did not receive Love
Is the degree to which we violently push it
Away.

Not realizing that Love *is* what Heals
And *Feeling* is *Healing*.

Instead, we all know of pain,
The pain of Non-Love.
Oh, how intimately we know this pain!
We *dare* not feel.

Instead,
We run.
We hide.
We bury.
We put on masks.

Until one day,
The dam bursts,
The walls crumble,
And we cry out for Love,
Not knowing *We Are Love*.

In our grief,
A small crack from the
Walls surrounding our heart
Births
The Truth.

If we dare look
We will see...
A Glimmer of our Truth.

Beckoning us gently
Like a mom to a babe,
She whispers,
"Shhh, young one,
Rest your weary head,
You are love. You are love."

And we say,
"Why did you abandon me?!
Where have you been!?"

Rocking us gently
She smiles,
"Always have I been here, beloved—
Awaiting this day.
You have been walking this life asleep,
My child!

It is time to Awaken".

-Discovering Divine Mother-

Come Back!

"Come back! Come back!
Wake up! I need you!
I need your Light!
Your joy! Your love!
Your zest for life!"
I cry out with the anguish
Tormenting my heart.

"I'm so sorry I buried you so deep
That, now,
I cannot even reach into the depths
To free you!

Without you,
I'm in a dungeon of darkness…
Imprisoned within myself.

And *you*, the key to my salvation—
Utterly lost!

Will we ever be reunited, my darling?"

-Words to the Lost Inner Child-

Writing is the Chisel

Tendrils of darkness
Encase and dim the Light within:
Stifling the gifts
That should overflow
From my core.

Rooted to the spot.
Fear and dread
Suffocate my
Divine Expression
Until it is barely perceivable…

Suddenly—
A whisper from the depths strikes a chord,
"Write, please, write!
It is the only way to free you!"

"I can't…."
I choke, feeling the gnawing in my gut
And lump in my throat,
"I feel paralyzed,
I'm not good enough.
I'm scared.
I'm unworthy.
I don't even know where to start!"

These menacing fears suffocate my
Divine Expression.
But still,
I hear the pleading, adamant whisper,

"Write...Write, I beseech you!"

"But..." and again the fears commence,
Tolling like an ominous bell
Their Assassinations
Of my Divine Expression.

"What if I never reach my potential?
What if I fail?
What if I try and no one cares or
I make no difference?
What if I'm seen and then
Everyone will know I'm a *nobody!*
What if I'm
Ridiculed?
Condemned?
Outcast?!"

"And,"
I wailed,
"That all means
I *really am*
Forgotten,

Abandoned,
Forsaken!
Banished from God!
Not loved by God!
I cannot—I will not!!!
I will NOT take one step further,
For I am afraid my worst fears are true!"

"My child," the voice assured,
"The only thing you have to lose
Are the fears you aren't
Worthy,
Loved,
And
In Grace.
You already are all those things.
Writing is the chisel that will chip away
All that isn't you—isn't Truth—
And will reveal all that has been there
All along.
Trust and write, beloved.
You are Love and Light,
And that can never be forsaken."

So, although I feel I'm being
Oppressed by these choking fears.

I write.

Worst Kind of Poverty

The feeling of having no purpose
Is the worst kind of poverty.
Robbing magnificent, creative souls
With the power to change the world
Of the knowing of the inalienable truth
That they are God.

Leaving desolate souls to live
A sense gratifying existence…
Like zombies just going through the motions
Getting the next "fix".
All to numb the pain and belief that
They are expendable and unimportant;
That they are separate.

I, too, know of this poverty.
Many days and nights it sucks
The Life,
The Joy,
The Love,
From me—
Bringing me to the brink of despair.

Weeping, I desperately scream to the Heavens,

"If I don't even feel or know my purpose,
How am I to heal this world?
How am I to complete my mission?
How am I to bring my brothers and sisters
Home?!"

And many times, no answer greets me
But the gentle whisper of spirit saying,
"Trust."

So, even though I feel broken, defeated, and
Ever still so lost,
I get up.
Take a deep breath.
And *choose* to love myself and others
A little more than I did yesterday.

-Trust-

Wanting More Answers

God, hear me! Why must I suffer?
I feel my heart is intertwined
With darkness and confusion.
When I pray
All I hear back is,
"Trust in me.
Accept all that is.
Patience, patience."

But I want to be healed now!
I want to come Home!
Why must I wait?!

"The greater the pain,
The greater the opportunity,
The greater the gift,
To help others tangled in
Webs of similar design."

But if I cannot see my own way
How am I to lead others?

"You already are.
And you will move more deeply
Into this Truth
By
Exploring
Asking
Trusting
Accepting
And choosing to leap
Despite the fear.

Have faith, my beloved,
You are so quick to want
To be where you are
Not…
That you are missing the gifts
Of being precisely who and where you are
Now."

-Heart to Heart with God-

But Why the Barriers?

Barriers, barriers, barriers!
Suffocating my will to go on.
Murdering my love for life.
Condemning my heart to

Pain.
Pain.
Pain.

I'm sick and tired of *pain!*
Of trying to build my *dreams,*
Only to be met with

BARRIERS.

Gatekeepers proclaiming
With a quirking, judgmental brow:

"You are not worthy.
You are not enough.
You are a failure.
Why are you still here, toiling away?
Everyone knows you don't have the drive!
You might as well not be here at all!"

And with a pounding thud
Of the gatekeeper's staff—

Here I am.

Questioning my worth,
Wondering why I'm alive at all!

What's the use?
All I see is
Pain.
Judgments.
Drudgery.

BARRIERS.

Pain rips open my core,
And I scream to the Heavens,
"Why the hell am I here!
Take me!
If this is what I have to be met with
Every time I take a step
Towards my dreams,
Take me now!
I can't do this!"

A crescendo of emotion

Overcomes me,

I weep,

With Anger.
With Pain.
With Resignation.

I whisper,
"Please, give me a sign…
Please tell me why…
Why the barriers?
Why does my heart and soul
Feel so *dead?*"

And as I quiet my mind to
Attune to my heart…
I hear:

"Barriers are created by the mind, beloved.
A closed door to your dream
Is merely a redirection to turn around
And see the window to God's dream
For you—
Where you can fly out into
The vast, open sky
Instead of walking through a door

With endless staircases.
Limitations do not exist
But where one creates them.
My child,
You are limitless.
You are infinite.
You have infinite potential.
The Gatekeeper is nothing but
A reflection of the beliefs
You hold against yourself
Making up a story as to why
A door was closed.
Those doors are closing
Out of Love for you
And redirecting you to see
The gift *you are*.
Once you do that—
You'll only see possibilities
Instead of limitations—
You'll see a vast, open, limitless sky
Instead of closed doors."

-Heart to Heart with God-

Mothering Me

I've always wanted to be a mother
But I'm waiting.
For I know I need to heal
These wounds within.

If I do not…
It will only create wounds upon my children
Too deep for a mother to heal.

If I deny *my inner child*
These wounds will only create
A wounded child in my children.

So, I am learning to mother me.

This first, I must do.

The Loss

How delicate our experience
Like the petals of a flower.
When storms ensue,
Uprooting our beloveds…
Leaving us
Crushed.
Broken.
Ripped wide open.
When we lose the Light of our Lives…
Why does the sun still rise?

-Beginning to Go Deeper into the Loss and Pain-

IV

The Cherished Guest

"The cure for the pain is the pain."

- Rumi

"These pains you feel are messengers. Listen to them."
- Rumi

The Pain

Pain is a great teacher
Often berated and ignored.

But if one takes the time
To ask pain, "Why are you here?
What is it I'm to learn?"

Then that's when

Pain,
Once looked upon as an intruder,
Becomes a most wise counselor.

Welcome pain as a most
Cherished Guest.
For she is merely
Illuminating the way
To greater Love.

Soothing the Pain and Chaos

I can't, I can't, I can't!
I'm not worthy!
I'm not good enough!
I feel I cannot take another step,
My heart is bursting from pain!
And I feel I don't know
Up from down.

I feel I'm a failure!
A nobody!
A lost cause!

Unseen!
Unheard!
Misunderstood!

My soul and heart want to soar,
But I'm encased in fear.
I feel like a worthless, meaningless
Caterpillar
Encased in tendrils of darkness
Dreaming of being a magnificent
Butterfly

Enveloped in Light.

I hate being a caterpillar.

I plea up to the Heavens,
"Please help—I need guidance!
My fear suffocates me!
I'm rooted to the ground...
My inner critic is eating
My inner child alive!
"You're stupid!
Good for nothing piece of shit!
No one wants you.
I never wanted you!
Wish you were never born!
You're weak and stupid!
I do not love you!"

These dark and slaying condemnations
Smolder my Divine Light...
ALAS, my will to live!
I want to disappear.
I want to escape. I even want to die!
Please help, God, if you are there,
Help me, please!"

I soothe the chaos in my mind and
Listen with my heart:

"We hear you, loved one. We are here.
We know your heart weighs heavy and
We are here to lift you up!
If only you could see how magnificent
You are.
You are already perfect.
You would not have to change one thing
To be more magnificent.
To be loved more.
To be worthy.

If you didn't change one iota,
You'd still be a most, wondrous
MIRACLE
For ALL to behold,
As we are beholding you now.

Weary one,
There is no need to earn or prove
Your worth—
Your worth to be seen
Or your worth to be loved!
Take refuge in the truth that you ARE
Already all THAT you wish to be!
Believe in yourself, and you will see this
Truth reflected to you.
Seeing is not believing.
Believing is seeing."

-Heart to Heart with God-

"P.S. Caterpillars are magnificent, too,
And have much to teach
If you listen carefully.
Enjoy the journey!"

The Miracle

Yearning,
Claws my heart
Burns my soul.

Suffocated expression.

Yearning to create,
Create and heal the world.

But, still, fears entrap me
In their grasp,
Sometimes I hate myself
And this self-imposed prison!

What do I do, God?
I feel like such a failure—
Always dreaming…
But never manifesting
My dreams into reality.

"Beloved, remember it is
About the journey
Each step,
Those that are excruciating to take,

And those that flow,
All a Gift,
All a Lesson,
All an Opportunity to Love—
To be Love, Love yourself, and
Love others!

Ultimately,
You are a creator in every moment!
As you learn to trust,
Follow your heart,
And
Choose into each moment,
You'll create from a
Space of Love
Instead of a
Place of Fear.
And that, beloved,
Is where the
Journey of life
And
All its flavors are
Experienced as
The Miracle."

-Heart to Heart with God-

Growing from an Experience of Non-Love

Nonlove overcame me,
Towards those who play the Victim:
"Why? Why can't you just change?
Why can't you take
Accountability for your life?"

Always getting triggered
By these actors who play
The Victim Role,
I'd turn away from them.
Condemn them.
Judge them.
Harshly abandon them—

Not looking...
Not digging for why I
Pushed these people away.

Finally, after experiencing this
Nonlove,
I realized they were bringing up a
Belief about myself.

When I "play" the Victim…
I despise myself.
I condemn myself.
I bury myself.

It is unacceptable!
It is WRONG!

Expressing this towards myself
A key piece was revealed,
How could *We*,
Powerful, magnificent beings
Of Love and Light,
Turn away from
Our Power?
Our Love?
Our Responsibility as Creators?
To become a Victim?

This was sacrilegious to me!
It awoke deep, suppressed, heart-wrenching
Pain within my core—
From I presume,
Lifetimes where the human race
Began forgetting their true nature:
The Fall of Grace.

I poured my aching heart into

Divine Mother's lap,
First expressing my rage
And then grieving this terrible loss.

As I was sobbing, asking,
"Why? Why? How could we turn away
From this knowing?
Why are we so lost?
I've probably wasted tons of lifetimes
Playing the Victim!"

She gently chuckled,
Smiled lovingly into my eyes
And said,
"Beloved, but for no other reason
Than Love.
Nothing is a waste.
Everything is a lesson and gift.
Being lost is an illusion—don't you see?
Never can one be truly lost.
One simply believes one is lost
Which creates the illusion of
Not knowing one's true nature.
One is simply playing a role
To know oneself
As Love.
Love is the answer and
These human experiences allow one to

Refine and face the fears and the lies,
Proclaim what is true,
And choose into ever greater
Love and Non-attachment,
What better way to know ourselves as Love
Than to experience its opposite, Non-love?"

I wept even harder, realizing the
Truth of these words.
Then I began laughing—We are Love!
We are Love! What a gift this has been!

I am at peace.

-Embrace with Divine Mother-

But Why the Cruelty?

My heart often feels
It will wither and die
From witnessing the injustices
Committed Upon Mother Earth.

God, why? Why am I here?
It is Hell on Earth!
I yearn for Heaven to
Descend upon this Earth!

There are days I'm afraid I'll lose
My heart.
My connection to Heaven.
Only to become a hardened shell
With no regard or reverence for life.

But, alas, I was born skinless.
And my capacity to feel
Cannot allow my heart
To die.

A blessing and a curse—
This Gift.

For as my heart tears and rips apart from
The hate, anger, cruelty, and injustice,
And wants to shut off
To never feel again…

It opens even more to
Envelop the whole world
In Love and Light!

As it is breaking and full of pain,
So, too, is it ever expanding into
Greater Love.

Maybe my brokenness…
Humanity's brokenness…
This Great Pain
When Transmuted,
Will create a Rainbow Bridge of Love
Heralding the Arrival of Heaven on Earth?

-Believing that Everything is a Gift-

V

Befriending the Shadows Within

"What hurts you, blesses you. Darkness is your candle."
— *Rumi*

"Do not worry if all candles in the world flicker and die. We have the spark that starts the fire."

— *Rumi*

Facing the Fears of the Self

O seeker,

The Gateway to Illumination
Is often gained only by facing the

Fears of the Self.

This, my dear one,
Is done by traversing courageously
To the depths of the Self,

Sealed and Forbidden.

Be not afraid of the shadows
Nor the banished parts of the Self,
For these forlorn parts hold the greatest key
For you to realize your Light.

Shunning and banning only creates more
Darkness,
Embracing, allowing, and loving brings
Light.

Face your fears
And walk courageously into the darkest,
Most feared parts of you,
And there you will discover,

Illumination.

And will be granted wisdom
To walk in this world
As a beacon for others—

Others trapped in their own versions
Of darkness.

Being Seen

I'm scared, God!
I'm afraid of my power.
I've always been
Invisible and insignificant and
To imagine being seen and important
Is terrifying!

What if I let everyone down?
At least if I'm invisible
No one will see me fall.

"But, beloved, you already are seen
And inspire the hearts of many!
They just haven't met you in the sense
Of 'meeting' you."

How is that possible?

"Through the fabric of the Universe,
Everything is possible,
Everything is shared,
Everything is seen.
Heart to heart, you've inspired many,
And many have inspired you."

But, I want to give up!
I want to be left alone!
I hate this turmoil in my heart and soul
That will not let me be!
I feel I'll never be good enough.

"Beloved, you are already magnificent.
We are just patiently waiting for you to
See this truth.
Then will be the time to light
The Torch of Truth for you to lead others—
To lead others out of their darkness
Into the warm embrace of Love—
Just as we are leading you."

-Heart to Heart with God-

The Spirit of Play

What am I to learn from failure, God?

"Patience, love, and joy in just being.
Failure is an illusion
And is designed to help you
Spark self-worth
In all that you are.
The endless struggle to have to
Achieve something to gain your worth
Is fruitless and impermanent.
It will only fan the flame of creation in you
But will not source it.
This, my beloved, must come from within.
The joy—the inner knowing so deep
You can see you already are
All you wish to be…
That when you create
From a Space of Joy,
It doesn't matter who listens.
Set fire to your own soul and in this
You'll spark a fire in others' hearts
Without even the strain and
Burden of struggle.

It is then you are free.
The Spirit of Play is
What will fan
Your Flame.
And in this there exists
No Failure.
Go out and play."

-Heart to Heart with God-

Bring the Shadow Sides Home to Reign As the Sun

I'm so afraid!
Fear consumes my will,
Silences my truth,
Darkens my hope.

I so want to be a mother.

But I cannot even conquer
My fear to live each day—
To see the gift
To go for my dreams!

Sometimes I cannot even get out of bed.
Sometimes I can't even make dinner
For myself—
Let alone brush my hair!

How can I achieve my dreams
When the shadow parts of me
Command my attention
And take center stage?

They say to me,

"It's not possible.
You'll never be anything.
It's scary out there!
Just play it safe!
You don't have what it takes.
Life is hopeless.
You are unworthy.
You are too sensitive.
You can't! You can't! You can't!"

These voices reign and
Try as I might to silence them—I collapse.

Willpower— it seems I lack.
It is a seed that has yet to take root
Within me.

Will I ever feel powerful?
Will I ever conquer fear?
Will I ever fall in love with life
To write a story
Of Love, Grace, Beauty and Magic,
Instead of writing and rewriting this story
Of Fear, Collapse, Struggle, and Strain?

Will the Light aspects of me ever

Reign to create my dreams?

God, please!? What do I do?

"Embrace the hurt. Embrace the fear.
Embrace the pain. Embrace the shadows.
Befriend and love these
Shadows part of you!
These parts, my love, are where the gift lies.
Instead of shunning and trying to 'rid of,'
Embrace, accept and nurture.
Listen and love.
This will open the doors to bring
These shadow sides Home
To reign as the Sun."

-Heart to Heart with God-

Only I Have the Key

I feel my gift is dead,
And it's anger keeping me from my
Salvation.

Anger at God—
Or, is it at myself?
Why am I here
If I keep coming back to Hell within?

Where is the solace?
It all seems like a battlefield—
With no hope of peace.

My own shadows are too dark to save.
I'm a poor excuse of a way-shower!
Pitiful and never enough.

These lies I believe…
Until my mission is thwarted
And I'm battling me.

Never set free.

But,

Only I have the key.

But where?
God, where?

"Listen cherished one,
Breathe and relax into me.
You are at battle with yourself
So much so,
You cannot
Hear me,
See me,
Feel me.
Nonetheless, I am here.
Constant as the sun.
Even when I wane
And the night overcasts its
Blanket of shadows,
I burn eternally
Beaconing You Home.
When the sun sets and night triumphs
Know that dawn is not far from its birth.
Yet, what you do not acknowledge
Is that as the sun sets, it does not die;
It is merely not within your perception—
Just as your Light is forever burning within
Awaiting your eyes to open.
Remember, the night has its gifts,

And those gifts are
Just as precious as the
Sun.
All is in perfection.
The moon, the sun, the dark, the light—
All are Sacred.
All serve a purpose.
Experience and cherish the gifts
Each one has to offer.
And in so doing,
You honor
All Aspects of yourself.
Everything you see is
You.
And this…

Is the Key.

*This is walking in this world
With your Eyes Wide Open."*

-Heart to Heart with God-

Befriending the Shadows

How do I become inspired by love?
How do I create?
I feel I'm forever going to be run
By fear and doubt!
Fear and doubt leave already!
You are not welcome here!

"But I'm afraid!
I need you to be my friend!"
I hear a tiny voice plead.

"Who are you?" I ask.

"I'm You— I'm just lost...
Will you hold my hand?
Will you show me the way?
I'm afraid of being afraid."

"Oh, my darling, it is ok to be afraid!
Let us walk together.
Being afraid is ok...
Even I get afraid sometimes!"

"You do?"

"Of course!
And you know what it's called
To move forward
Even when you feel afraid?"

"No, what?"

"Courage!
And when Courage befriends Fear,
Courage helps Fear to see
That all there is...
Is Love.
Courage is the Sun that
Shines so brightly
That the more we use it,
The more shadows
Find their way Home.
We awaken to the truth
That the shadows
Were just an experience
To bring us to Love."

"But how?"

"Love is so bright that even shadows
Will one day discover themselves
To be just as bright as Love.
But you have to befriend the shadows,

So that they take off their marauder cloaks
And discover how
Bright they Truly Are.
Then they reunite with the
One Love
To shine as a Beacon
To bring all confused shadows Home."

"What happens when there are
No more shadows?"

"We discover all there ever was
And all there ever will be
Is Love."

-Reuniting with a Shadow Aspect of Myself-

VI

Liberated

"You have heard that it was said, 'Love your neighbor and hate your enemy.' But I tell you, love your enemies and pray for those who persecute you."
  - Jesus Christ, Matthew 5: 43-44

"How you access compassion is by seeing the world through other people's eyes."

- Louix Dor Dempriey

I, Alone, Am Responsible

You were a child once, innocent and free,
How did *you* get so "broken"?
Your "brokenness" created patterns,
And those patterns you passed down to me...
You have a beautiful child within,
Lost in the dark, too!
We are not so different, you and I.
There is no one to blame.
There is no one to blame.
I am responsible for *my* Healing.
Just as you are responsible for *yours*.

-Inner Mullings to Those that Gifted Me the Opportunity To Be Love-

Forgiveness

Beginning to see through the eyes of love,
I see the chains that bind,
I choose to forgive.
I choose to forgive.
Set free.

The Angel Behind the Pain

Forgive me,
Ones I've hurt,
For
Playing the Victim…
For
Blaming you
For everything…

My eyes are open.
You did the best you could
With what you knew.
How can I
Hold that against you?

Pain has a funny way
Of leading
All
Of
Us
To be someone
We don't want to be.

Let us, together,

Have compassion
For one another.

Let us choose to see
The
Angel
Behind
The
Pain.

Rejection is Merely an Invitation

Especially when you reject me,
I see this as a most blessed gift:
An invitation.

For no one is to blame.

There is a lesson in the rejection—
Often obscured by the external battle
Of proving ones worth!

Oh, but beloved, this is illusion!

As within, so without.

I accept this invitation and
I dare to pull off the veil of inauthenticity.

I realize this circumstance
Is seeded by my doubts
Of my own self-worth.

And this one who "rejected"
Is merely shining a light—

A light that penetrates to my core to
Unearth hidden, non-loving aspects of me.

How grateful I am to this one for
Being the Catalyst

The catalyst for me to proclaim this day,
"I am worthy!
I am Love!"

To delve into my own heart and soul
Unearthing all non-love within me,
So that I may refine, heal, and become
Ever closer to…

Embodying the Creator's Perfect Love.

"I am a Champion of the Light.
And each day I choose to
Delve deeper and deeper into my heart
To Become Greater Love."

Projection

For all this time I've been
Looking at myself.
Everything is me!
Everything can be healed inside me!
When you want to heal a part of your being,
You do not stand in front of a mirror
And fix the reflection.
You heal the part of yourself that is creating
The reflection!

Everything is Within You

Seeking, seeking, seeking
But never finding God.

How can one find that which one already is?

The seeker seeks oneself.

Much like one tries to find the
Sunglasses that are on her person,
Never finding it outside herself
But once discovering it upon her crown

Chuckling because it was there all along!

Remembrance of Self cannot be found
With seeking this or that with an air of need.

Remembrance of Self *must* be found
By opening up to the Truth
That everything you are searching for
Is
Within
You.

Liberation

If We are All One
Then What I Awaken Within Me
Leads to the potential
For Awakening
Within
Us All.
The Potentiality for Growth
When we courageously
Step Forth
To Shine our Light and
Refine our Being
Is Infinite.
When One's Shadows Within
Are Brought forth to the Light
It Creates an Opportunity
For All
To Awaken
Their Shadows to the Light,
It Paves the Way for Liberation.

We All Have the Key.

*-We All Have Within Us the Power to
Choose to Become Greater and Greater Love.*

*What Greater Gift Could We Give,
Than this Refinement of our own Being?-*

VII

Remembering Together to Bring Us Home

"I wish I could show you when you are lonely or in darkness the astonishing light of your own being."
						- Hafez Shirazi

"Stop acting so small. You are the universe in ecstatic motion."

- Rumi

Infinite Love

Oh, how my heart longs
To express this Love:
Boundless, infinite,
All-encompassing LOVE!

I want to shout with joy,
Stand on the rooftops
And wrap my arms around
All the aching hearts
Proclaiming,
"We are LOVE!
Come Home! Come Home!"

A longing within me,
An aching sigh,
To hold those hurting hearts…
To show them their Light.
To free all those aching hearts
So that they may be
The Infinite Love
That they are.

-Do You Hear Me, beloveds?-

Opportunity

The greatest gift
We can give humanity
Is to become greater Love.

From one breath to the next
We can choose to be greater Love
And align to our
Divine Authentic Expression.

No matter what we've done,
How many times we've made
Less than loving or *even* cruel choices,
Or if we chose to be cruel
Even five minutes ago,

We have this most blessed opportunity!

Now the question is, my friend,
Will you take it?

Builder of our Castle in the Sky

We all have inside us
A little child who's been hurt.
Our inner critic often berates and
Condemns this innocent part of us.

When we do finally talk to
Our inner child with love,
The child shies away,
Walls around her heart.

It is then that we must be patient,
Loving and kind,
To take down the wall

Stone
by
Stone

Memory
by
Memory

To give the inner child,

Which is the creator of our dreams,
Wings to soar!

To free this Dreamer
to be
The
Builder of our
Castle in the Sky!

-From Saboteur to Dream-Maker-

Allow the Unfolding

"Why can't it just happen?
Aren't I worthy?
Don't I matter?"

Allow the Unfolding.

Especially when you experience rejection,
You are a champion!
This is a most precious gift
Offered to you on a silver platter
By your own soul.
Don't you see?

It is inviting you to see yourself
As a diamond in the rough.
Only you can uncover
The gem that you are
For all to behold.
This is done by you discovering
And knowing deep within your core—
Your worthiness.

Once you experience this revelation
Of your worth,

Then the world will reflect this
Truth.

*-Everything is a Mirror
Everything is You-*

Love is the Language of the Universe

Breathe deeply, young one
Tread not in fear,
But in Love.

Love is the language of the Universe.
Send ripples of Love from your Heart
To those parts of you that are most wounded
And to the parts of the world
That are the same.

For Both are One.
And you, blessed emissary of Light,
Are the Universe.

Sending Love to yourself
Is sending Love to all others,
And sending Love to others
Is sending Love to yourself.

What a beautiful mosaic this truth creates,
As within, so without.

-We Are All Connected-

Every Thought You Have Is a Seed

We create our own reality,

This is Truth.

Yet, deep within we often
Feel powerless...
How can this be?

The thoughts we have entertained
Have served to disempower us,
To bring darkness,
To blind us from our potential.

Yet, many of us still hear
That small voice within—
Yearning, yearning, yearning
For reunion with the Truth.

Even still,
It has been so hard to fight
The booming voice of condemnation
And criticism—
The one that tears us down and

Is full of skepticism.

"How, God, do we create the magical life
We know is possible
Yet struggle to embark upon?
How do we overcome the dark forces
That appear to be pulling us under
In a sea of illusion and disempowerment?
What are we to do?"

"We hear your pleas, blessed ones.
We offer you this:

Every thought you have is a seed
And the degree of focus upon such thoughts
Will determine what fruit you will bear—
For energy and time spent on negativity
Only creates the same.

So dear ones,
With each critical thought,
Plant, instead, a seed of encouragement
And unconditional love,

With skepticism,
Plant, instead, a seed of wonder
And anticipation of the majesty
Of what is right in front of you,

With pessimism
Plant, instead, a seed of all the possibilities
Of what could go right,

And with disappointment
Plant, instead, a seed of magic, wonder,
And faith.

But be patient…
As it takes time, persistence,
And continuous love
To reprogram your state of consciousness,
Just as it does to tender
A seed into sprout,
A sprout into a sapling,
And sapling into a tree.
What is most empowering to know
Right now…
Is that in every single moment
You have a choice
Of what to fertilize and create.
Will you choose Love or Fear?

Fear is the lie. Love is the truth.

And the dark forces
That you describe as pulling you under
Have only been created

By the fear-based thought forms
You have given credence to
And can be transmuted into Love
At your request and focus—
All is You and *nothing is separate.*
Where you place your focus
Is what will take root.

Envision the possibilities of everything
Being exactly as it is meant to be—
Because it is.
Envision yourselves as perfect just
As you are—
Because you are.

Align with this truth and you are free."

-The Answers are Within Each and Every One of Us-

What Would Love Do?

Know now,
You Are Powerful.
You Are Worthy.
You Are Love.
You Are Magnificent.
You Are the Creator.
There is nothing to fear.
You are free to be free.
To create just to create.

Love yourself.
See your perfection.
Be and choose to be
The authentic You.

I hear so many of you ask,
"But what if I am not enough?
What if I make a mistake?
What if I am not accepted?
What if I self-sabotage?"

And we say to you,
"It is not a race.
You are where you are

And it's divinely perfect.
Remember you are a creator
And can change any moment you choose.
One moment you choose victimhood,
The next mastery.
Refine and *choose to be willing to choose*
Mastery more and more
And you will draw to you
The perfect circumstances to grow.
Don't worry yourself
With how or when or if you've made it
As these are from the ego mind
And only serve to blind you
From the truth of who you are.
Simply live by asking
'What would Love do?' And do that."

-*The Answers Within*-

Create from this Space

What makes your heart sing?
What makes you jump out of bed
In the early hours
Where it's still dark and dance barefoot
Along the cold floor?
What spurs that fire in your belly?
That yearning in your soul?
That hope in your being?
Create from the space within you
That finds joy and ecstasy
From simply *being*.
This is the space that
Moves Mountains.
Parts Seas.
Creates Miracles.
This is the space that
Brings you Home.

You are a Wayshower

Losing hope for humanity
Is easy to do.
The Darkness.
The Despair.
The Crime.
The Cruelty.
All seem like too much to bear
For a heart so gentle.

Young one, have faith!

For having a gentle heart
In a cruel world
Is a gift beyond measure.

Those who are *most cruel*,
Are also the *most lost*.
They need our love *most desperately*.

Pray for these, young one,
Reflect back their Light and Love
And help to bring them Home!

For you,

Wayshower!

Earth Angel!

Are meant to stir the hearts of those
In the DARK.

To be a beacon,
A LIGHT,
To guide the lost ones
Into the Remembrance that
They, too, are Love.

VIII

Our Homecoming

*"Gaining awareness is the access to power.
Applying awareness is the attainment of power."*
- Louix Dor Dempriey

"Close your eyes. Fall in love. Stay there."

- Rumi

The Time-Capsule

Coming Home to the
Truth and Magnificence
Of One's Divinity
Is carefully seeded through one's life,
Through circumstances, words, challenges,
And mere, mundane occurrences.

But it is nothing short of miraculous!

A Miraculous Alchemy of the Heart
To spring forth a
Remembrance of Truth.

To Awaken,
Life sends us experiences
Perfectly orchestrated
To bring us into our own hearts:
The Portal to Our Divinity.

These are the most Sacred Time Capsules—
Divine Alchemical Promptings
That bring Us Home,
That guide Us back into the
Heart of the One.

Gift of the Rainbow

Eyes to the skies
Dreaming
Of what awaits
At the rainbows end.

"What awaits there?"
We all wonder and dream,
Losing sight of the gifts
Before our eyes.

Our eyes to the skies
We do not see
The gift of the rainbow
Is at our feet.

-Gratitude Will Light the Way-

Mastery

Mastery, Beloved, is what will lead to
The Homecoming.

Mastery is equally accepting
The ugly and the beautiful.
The challenges and the grace.
The pain and the pleasure.

For there can be pain,
But not suffering if
One sees the pain as a gift—
As an opportunity.

Everything is a blessing.
Everything has meaning.
Everything is a gift.

Rejoice and see the perfection
In all imperfection!

That is freedom!
That is when one breaks free from
The chains of illusion
And opens the door to Grace.

The Oasis of Our True Self

There are many times we may feel we are
Wandering
Wandering
Wandering
Aimlessly in a desolate desert.

How do we get to a place
Of accepting and allowing the flow of life
To take us on the Wings of the Divine,
To fill our spirit with a renewed sense of purpose,
To taste the waters of Divine love?

The Oasis we so long for is within
Each of Us.

The path through the desert to the Oasis
Can only be tread with Love.
Every dying tree,
Every worn bush,
Every tired creature,
Embrace with Love and proclaim:
"I love you. I love you.

Please forgive me for creating
This desert within myself."

Love is the rain that will heal
The desert of
Desolation,
Fear,
Darkness,
And Pain.

Love is the answer.
Love will wash away all that binds Us
From the Oasis that is our True Self,

The Seat of our Homecoming.

IX

Of One Heart

"I have been a seeker and I still am, but I stopped asking the books and the stars. I started listening to the teaching of my own Soul."

-Rumi

"Your heart knows the way. Run in that direction."
                                                    - Rumi

The Student and Master

The Student:
"But I want to be healed now!
I want to be everything I am supposed to be,
So I can do what I was sent here to do!"

The Master:
"What if I told you that
You already are whole and perfect
And everything you are to be?
You came here
To learn to love
All of It
And
All of You."

The Song

Entangled in darkness
I sought for the Light within,
There I met
A girl in pain.

In this abyss
I discovered her.
She was in pain and despair,
Reaching out her hand,
Tangled in webs of darkness.

Although this apparition
Appeared scary and dark.
I clasped her hand,
Lifted her up,
And unbound her from the dark webs.

She looked frail and afraid,
Covered in mud and muck and
Shards of broken glass.

Empathy flooded my heart,

Gingerly I…
Tended to her wounds,

Washed her from the stain and grime,
Brushed back her hair
And looked into her eyes.

Falling.
Falling.
Falling.

A Galaxy of Love and Light
I fell into her eyes.

A Portal of Love erupted from
My heart to hers,
There we truly met for the first time.

Suddenly…
I was struck by a most beautiful melody—
Unlike any I've heard.

The voice of an angel,
So gentle—yet riveting!
It cascaded over my being,
And filled me with buzzing Light and Love
Till I overflowed.

I wept…
I breathed deeply…
This Surrender

Into
Love.

In this space,
I Knew
The
Truth.

The girl in pain,
Is me—
Her song unsung.

The song…
It is our song—
Our message to the world.
It cries out in earnest to be
Shared.

And I know,
At the *very* center of my being,
I must step forth and share it,
For it is the only way to

Set Us Free.

-Time to Step Out into the Light-

Of One Heart

Goodbyes are the doorway to
The One.
Have you ever noticed that
If you truly say goodbye to another
Your heart
Breaks?

But in this

Breaking

Is a

Renewing

And the Truth that we are

ALL ONE.

Goodbyes are Not Forever,
For We are All of One Heart.

So, as I come to wish you farewell,
May I only leave rose petals in your hearts,
As you have only left rose petals in mine.

I thank you for
All the lessons, the tears, the laughter,
THE LOVE!

I say goodbye to you, beloveds
With only love emanating from my being…

And I wish you to know,

This is not truly goodbye—

For,
The lessons learned and
The hearts touched,

Are of
One Learning
And
One Heart.

And I take with me

These Rose Petals of Love,
All the Days of my Life.

So…
As you and I close these pages,
Know we are never apart,

As I bow to you in reverence
You forever remain in my heart.

Namaste.

Afterword

Sending Energetic Ripples Through All That Is

Dear Fellow Wayshower,

Yes, you are a Wayshower, an Earth Angel, an Emissary of Light!

Please do not doubt your worth.

You matter.

You are meant to be here.

You are significant.

You are a gift to this world.

So, we've come to the end of this poetry book. *We made it, you and I.* I'd like to express my utmost gratitude for you taking this journey with me. What a gift you have given! I am beyond grateful to have had the privilege of sharing my vulnerability, pain, hope, and love with you. Although we may not have met in the sense of "meeting"—we know one another in our heart of hearts and know, intimately, our pain of pains. Thank you!

Before this journey comes to a close, I would like to share one last message with you. I pray you find comfort in these words.

During one of my more doubtful moments where I found myself wondering what my purpose in life is, I decided to do a meditation. I asked God, "What am I to do today to touch the world in a positive way?" I had the divine inspiration to start writing down what I was receiving through my thoughts. The message I received, inadvertently, led me to start writing poetry. It was a catalyst that gave me permission to delve into my hurt and pain and write the poems that are a part of *May I Only Leave Rose Petals* even before I knew it would become a book. I would like to share the message that came forth with you, for it does not just speak to me, but all of us:

What are you to do today?

Take the journey within, beloved. Learn your divine

nature. Practice peace, joy, and mindfulness. Expand your consciousness.

This is where your journey begins. It begins by being present with yourself and allowing, accepting, being, and loving All of You. You are the master creator. This is where master creation begins. This seemingly small step is actually a giant leap. "You are not the drop in the ocean, but the ocean in the drop." – Rumi.

Do not think that you are not making brave steps forward by your meditative, self-awareness, and self-love practices, for this is one of the most courageous steps of your journey. You are touching the world through these steps.

Many people believe that to make great changes in the world that they must go out and do something: start a campaign, begin a charity, speak publicly, or be in the spot light. But, my wondrous child, daring to work invisibly by delving into the depths of your true self and intimately connecting with every aspect of who you are and confronting your shadow each day is the definition of bravery! It is paving the way for others to do the same.

Through this place of connection within yourself, you are more powerfully and more intimately connected to All and able to consciously help All.

There will come a time for you to be in a more (physically) visible place. What is important to know right now is that you are visible in a way that is imperceptible by many but is no less powerful than if you were out in the spotlight. For your light shines so brightly within that it touches all that is around you and speaks to hearts across eons.

Ultimately, by you doing your inner work and raising your vibration and consciousness, you are making a difference. Do not ever doubt that! When you go within to know yourself, when you catch a negative thought and change it to a positive thought, when you are aware of and take responsibility for your energy, when you consciously choose to send love and see love wherever you go… You are the ocean in the drop that is released, sending energetic ripples through all of THAT IS.

So you ask, how can you touch the world today? What do you need to do?

Be loving and patient with yourself.

Find what nurtures your soul.

Celebrate your steps forward.

Be not discouraged when you fall. This, too, is a gift.

Understand that there are many changes taking place beneath the surface—changes that you are largely unaware but that will cumulate into a beautiful manifestation of creation.

Know, without a shadow of a doubt, you have already touched countless hearts. If only you could see how many hearts you've touched across the eons you'd be overcome with the majesty of your own Light and Beauty—just as we are overcome right now.

And finally, we invite you to have faith the size of a mustard seed, beloved, for, indeed, you have the power to move mountains.

May You be Blessed,

J.S. Drake, aka, Jessi

About the Author

J.S. Drake, a native to Torrington, WY, is a substance abuse counselor currently residing in Ogden, UT with her family. J.S. Drake has been a closet poet most of her life until she was inspired to share her poetry with others through the creation of *May I Only Leave Rose Petals*. This is just the beginning as J.S. Drake hopes to continue inspiring people through her poetry.

If you feel moved and wish to share these messages with others, the author has created a platform on Facebook and Instagram for readers to reach out, interact, share their own messages and higher truths, and share the messages of *May I Only Leave Rose Petals*.

You may reach the Facebook page by searching
@MayIOnlyLeaveRosePetals
or through the link:
www.facebook.com/MayIOnlyLeaveRosePetals/

You may reach the Instagram page by searching
mayionlyleaverosepetals
or through the link
www.instagram.com/mayionlyleaverosepetals/

The author also invites readers to email her at
mayionlyleaverosepetals@gmail.com.
She would love to hear any feedback and messages
readers wish to share.

www.ingramcontent.com/pod-product-compliance
Lightning Source LLC
Chambersburg PA
CBHW030117100526
44591CB00009B/426